I have secrets......Does he love me too

J.Penny

All rights reserved by J.Penny. This book or any portion thereof may not be reproduced or used in any manner whatsoever without the expressed written permission of the publisher except for the use of brief quotations in a book review.
ISBN: 978-0-578-92806-7
Distributed by Power Of Purpose Publishing
Www.PopPublishing.com
Atlanta, Ga. 30326
All rights owned and reserved by J. Penny

Dedication

This is dedicated to the LGBTQ community
and anyone else with iniquities that struggle with knowing
that even with our secrets
God still loves us.
I too
am just like you.
This is from me,
for me,
and this is for you.

Biography
I am

Who am I.......
Who am I?
I am a ball of built up tension, anger, cries, and sexual desire.
General desire to inspire the greatest to be awakened.
Selfishly
I want to be acknowledged for it all.
Will it be enough recognition?
OF COURSE NOT!
The self-loving parts of me know I deserve so much more.
The money, the gold, the love, now that's a reward,
because I can be materialistic, statistically rightfully so.
I'm not a hoe,
but I want Love from all the right and wrong places.
The spaces that could be available if I wasn't so abundantly filled.
I am filled with laughter, affirmations, and deep conversations that could last till the sun rises and dries the morning dew.
I am sometimes confused about everything that exists, but I also like pieces of my ignorant bliss,
because I am a tourist or an adventurous explorer to all the unknowns.
It excites me.
My past is my crutch and my excuse to receive the attention I long for, for someone to take care of me, but not for too long, cause see after a while I am long gone to the next thrill.
I can send chills down your spine whether it's from my sensual sexuality or my spiritual prosperity.
It's really yours to choose, because I'm the type with numerous elements you can pull me out of.
I am a drug.
Rather you like it or not you can get addicted, and I feed off that shit.

Like me, love me, or hate me it all works the same.
The fascination is all a game I use to entertain.
What escape can I take us to?
I am my own fantasy I invite you to see.
It's exotic and unique.
Chakras perfectly progressing and complete.
I like to be spoiled.
I like to tease.
I also like to be pleased.
Who am I?
I am Penny.

Table of Contents

INTRODUCTION	1
CHAPTER 1: SECRET PLEASURES	3
CHAPTER 2: PROMISCUOUS GIRL PROBLEMS	13
CHAPTER 3: DARK TIMES OF PAIN AND SUFFERING	23
CHAPTER 4: THE MOTIONS OF THE CONDEMNED , AND CONVICTED	39
CHAPTER 5: WHEN YOU FALL FOR LOVE	53
CHAPTER 6: ….AND WHEN IT CRASHES INTO YOU	60
CHAPTER 7: MANIPULATED AND MANIPULATOR	78
CHAPTER 8: THE SPIRITUAL REALM	89

Introduction

Am I Good Enough For You Poetry?
What do you call it when you forgive someone, but what they did still brings you pain?
I'm not trying to place blame or pick a fight,
I just want to express my hurt to you.
I want to let you know what I'm going through and I love you;
but some of your words and the lack thereof has hindered me
from rising above my inadequacies.
Some said things that has stuck with in
and caused me to walk away from my pen a time or two.
I just wonder how far I would have gone if I got support from you.
Writing has always been my weapon to win understanding.
Something that made me feel proud,
and maybe I would speak my words out loud if only you were interested when I wrote them down.
If only you blessed me with courage and introduced me to my worth.
Maybe me and poetry wouldn't feel like strangers.
When we reunite,
I invite her to watch me get exposed privately
to make sure that my right to be acquainted with her is valid.
Yes, I was almost ashamed of my talent.
"Writing doesn't really make money to pay my bills", so sometimes I'd forget that I'm good at this skill.
Sometimes I thought I was too good for this skill.
Sometimes I feel like this skill is too good for me.
Tell me.
Am I good enough for you poetry?

Speak to Me Poetry

Speak out!
Speak through!
Make yourself known and tell the truth!
Touch my heart!
Touch theirs!
Inspire and encourage!
Make your words an epic affair!
Initiate change!
Spark the reader!
Open up to me!
I am so very eager to connect with you
to have a new respect for you
to check for you on a consistent basis,
and have substance to fill the blank spaces in my notes
in my mind
in my writer's block that drives me to give up some days;
but I have so much to say about the world
About violence
or being gay.
I have so much to say;
so talk back to me
educate me
and recreate with me.,
Be bold with me! Take control of me! Reach back out to me as I reach into you.
Grab hold of me, or let me through; because I want you and everything that you could possibly help me be.
I want to write you down or speak you out.
Please!
Speak to me poetry.

Chapter 1:
Secret Pleasures

When I'm upset I want sex, so could you just sex me,
and wet me up with your hands and lips?
Touch and kiss my body with every chance you get
with a few hickies to plant so I can reminisce.
Fuck me gently so I can forget
the emptiness you have to leave me with.

There's a weakness in my flesh, and I just
can't let go of it.
My body is exposing it
in her eyes, there's a glow in it,
and my mind
I can't control it.
Sometimes I'm unashamed of this sin.
Sometimes I'm ashamed of this sin.
Sometimes I touch women skin,
and sometimes our juices blend.
I know it's a sin, and I know I keep this sin with me, but does that mean that your eyes can judge me;
because I dedicate my Sundays to the pulpit and the praise team and the pastors that preach, then
I dedicate my body to my lover in the sheets for the week.
Am I the only one that's conflicted with myself every day about my day and about my ways
and about the things in the back of my mind that I can hear God say, or the things in the back of my mind that I know my mother would say?
"Now Jazmyne, you know this is not his will," but never would she say that she would still love me anyway.
For I know her love will still show and it will still shine, and his love will still shine even if it interrupted my dark secrets that I decided to share on these pages.

There's a rage inside of me that's directed towards the other side of me.
I can't stand her.
She's just weak in her flesh. She likes to sleep in her mess, and I just can't let go of it. My body is showing it, in her eyes there's a glow in it. In her kiss there's so much love and I notice it.
It feels good against my pain. It's planted deeply in her veins, and I want it, so I go against the grain and love her back. But will God still have my back? He knows that discipline and self-control are the things that I lack.
That I'm the type of person that will shack up with her, wake up to her, feel her, and be held by her in this cold world where a love like hers feels definite.
On a daily basis, I can give you cases after cases where I look to find in the back of my mind that no one is good enough.
Then my head gets filled with all this guilt and stuff, which overwhelms me some days.
I try to change my ways and I still fall short some days and my court date is soon to come.
He knows my heart desires to reside in his kingdom.
I admit that I am weak, and the enemy succeeds in seeking me and my flesh, but I don't know how to begin to let go of it.
I enjoy every dose of it, but my soul fights against this.

I'm in love with my sin, and I put kisses on her skin, but then
I think about my sin and how my patience is running thin with myself,
because I know how much
trouble I am actually in.
I'm afraid.
I'm a sinner.
I'm weak.
Save me.

I opened my eyes at 4:35 and fantasized about you.
A million and one scenarios going through my head of how to lead you to my bed.
I guess I still have hope and my p**** will forever dream
of seeing you in between
and vice versa.
Are you ever curious about what it feels like?
For me to release what I have all over you
to kiss on and lick up all of your p**** juice
while rubbing on your thighs
gripping your ass until you climax.
Then turning you over to caress you down with my hands and lips.
I want to do this.
It's been on my to-do list for quite some time.
I think about it in my mind,
to hear you moan and feel you shake again and again.
I can't pretend that I don't want you
regardless of how much trouble it brings.
It was never said to be easy doing the right thing.

When I'm hitting up your phone
I get in this zone
and then I get to thinking
my juices get to dripping.
Words start to flow out my mouth.
Before you know it, I'm ready to show you what I'm about.
I can look in your eyes and tell you,
"yes"
to whatever gets our bodies together.
I don't need your forever's.
I enjoy your quickies.
Anything to hear your moans.
The fix I get in your kiss.
It started with them lips.
This feeling might not be for long, but I'm mesmerized by your tone.
 I should really leave you alone,
but I'm not ashamed to say it's something about you that makes me do wrong.

It's like an ecstasy pill you feed me.
With your sex appeal you tease me.
The distance from you is so tedious.
The skin you're in
I begin to envy
because it's where I want to be
Day in and out, these thoughts are taunting.
You have no idea how deep this wanting for you is.
Your body is above any compliment I could ever give.
The opportunity of your company
"baby where you want me" comes to mind.
See I'm tryna live out every fantasy
I have about you.
It's more frequent than I will ever admit to being true.
I lose count of how many trances you put me through
multiplied by ten when you say you want me again.
Don't play these games with me.
Your every word is tingling
especially
when it's concerning this intimacy.
Let's just keep this between you and me
and fulfill these dreams secretively.

Chilling on my couch and all I can think about
is you.
Now….
this ain't no love thing, but for you to be next to me,
lips within kissing distance
instead of this mental resemblance that presents itself whenever I close
my eyes.
I hear your moans when my head rolls
pretending to be between your thighs
sighs........
Damn, I wish I could have you at my leisure.

I don't go to church every Sunday.
Sometimes I like to stay home and not pretend and have my sorrows blend in the background of my happy stories.
No, sometimes I don't want to share my testimonies and hesitate to voice my prayer request to the gossip conferences on Monday mornings.
I'd rather roll up my blunt and speak about the beauties of this world.
I can't get up this morning to curl my hair and wipe off last night, because last night I was drowning in my memories of the choir director making a talk show of my lifestyle.
No smiles this Sunday forced in front of my step father's face cause I remember I saw him staring at me below my waist.
No, my trust in men has been replaced with this taste of sin every time she walks my way and brushes against this skin I'm in.
I'm hypnotized in her eyes, thinking about the cease of my thoughts when going in between her thighs.
Still, I rise to see there are no promises for the next day, so I try to pray anyway.
Now I'm caught in this world with multiple girls and numerous fixes between her lips is my addiction.
Can't seem to resist her attention, and it gets confusing in this dimension.
It's extremely amusing though I forget to mention.

Chapter 2:
Promiscuous Girl Problems

Can I be "That Girl"?
Can I be "that girl"?
The one that gets that boy.
Not the one to be toyed
with or picked up in dark places.
Not the one in the " friend zone", or
the one not good enough to be shown
around " that boy's" friends.
I want "that boy's" hands.
That boy that's pretty in the face and everywhere else.
Am I good enough?
Do I meet the requirements to get him to love me to his fullest extent
with the goodest intent.
First, I gotta catch his eye.
Tell me what does it take to get the handsome guy
It's more than just a nice face.
Do I need a smaller waist?
Should I get in shape?
Then after that, how can I keep his attention?
How do I get him to mention my name when
I'm not around?
What does he need when his mouth is frowned
When his world is down.

Am I capable of entering his heart?
Can I pull him out of the hard places life puts him into?
Will he tell me his story?
Can I give him a happily ever after?
Can I keep him focused
And steady?
Am I ready?
What would happen if I was that girl
and I got him?

Ever been in love before?
Not I.
I never said how I feel, or admitted to all my emotions towards no guy.
Never fell asleep on my lover's chest at night.
Never gave in and called it truths to stop a fight.
I never confessed to a fear of losing that one.
Never sat back and sunk in his love and just became one.
I never got comfortable with him one hundred percent.
Never said what I really meant
or meant what I really said.
No, I can't tell you about how we exchanged "I love you's" in bed.
When it comes down to letting love in, I'm not the biggest fan.
Well, at least not of the actual action, but the idea of it is attractive.
To hold each other down through the mist of anything at all.
Not being able to let go and show that I get weak for him is my biggest flaw.
I can't say that I tried.
I can't say that I haven't wondered why
this major issue keeps me up and my eyes wide at the latest hour.
The sweetest taste of love and I'll still turn sour.
I hate to be boastful of this bittersweet power.
The situation
I can't describe

my stubborn heart won't let them in.
The privilege to be in love with him,
I have never EVER been.

I saw you yesterday.
I saw you in a state that I could never be.
Shined in the light of her world, I saw your darkness.
All your secrets, flaws, and falls that you ever had.
I saw you and I called it beautiful.
From the cuts you never slit to the tears you never kissed for consolation.
A reputation you withhold being so brutal and so cold to mask your weakness.
You are bold, but I see you
and it's transparent
All your ways you try to keep distant.
 I know this is your line of defense but you are still near and clear to me.
Your purest love and your inner beauty I can still see.

Females are my escape from my male reality.
I know it's sad to have that mentality, but what is it that you want from me?
I know what's right and what's wrong
but I can't always keep my mind strong.
Living in this place of wherever or a different one
I need a getaway sometimes just for a little while.
I'm not in denial that I have a problem or a fix.
It's just something I used to cope with.
A vice just like the one you roll up
when getting ready for any day that you wake up to.
They are just here to help me get through,
so may I be excused
while I
light up?

I don't know about my tomorrows.
If I could borrow the future, then I would still miss the
in between things.
Cause the present itself
is still a blur
Even the things that reoccur don't manifest the same.
I claim a false power
displayed a false, sour, interpretation for our love.
I admit to all these things
and still knock on your door again
asking to let me in this time and maybe for a moment my heart will open,
but I don't know how long it's going to last.
This broadcast of my love for you is in contrast of the things I'm supposed to do.
Yet right now, that's not how I want to choose.
This current opportunity of having you I don't want to lose,
and the next point of time I can't say which side my mind will appeal to,
or what I'm willing to go through.

I enjoy feeling the same thing
more than one time.
I'm not ashamed to say you pop into my mind,
so smile
and be flattered
because you left a mark on me.

I carry it with me everywhere I go.
It shows, and it grows.
From the bitch that did me wrong to my love story all in one sad song.
I got baggage.
I'm supposed to be a savage, but I let each one reside inside my heart.
The trouble,
starts with the ones that mean me no good.
In the middle
there's the ones that could love me deeply.
I should give them a chance, but my hands carry this baggage.
I'm supposed to be a savage, but I keep each ex with me like a packrat.
And even though some could care less
I still have to have that memory
and desire to rekindle the fire with the people I need to retire from the frontal lobe of my brain.
I keep the chain of love affairs with no purpose in mind but to weep about the pain it caused me.
The time it has paused me from
believing that baggage meant something other than a lesson that I was once learning.

Chapter 3:
Dark Times of Pain and Suffering

I just want to shout, scream and weep
as if I was alone at the top of a mountain peak.
I want to throw, tear, and destroy everything in front of me.
But I can't show the world that I'm angry;
so my flesh trembles against my bones to keep my emotions secluded.
A glass of wine I wish I could use to dilute the outburst seeping out of my pores.
Anger.
Anger at the venomous flower that attracts my desire to touch.
Anger at the parental guidance that never showed me enough attention, help, belief.
So many things that fill me with an abundance of grief.
Angry at her for the lack of equal love to each.
Angry at him for not being around to teach me my worth.
Angry at myself for not having the courage to reach out for help.
I just left everything behind closed doors.
All of this anger and nobody knows,
and it travels deeper to where my depression goes,
and it consumes me some days and affects my fickle ways.
It clogs up my throat and boils my stomach in the worst way possible.
My teary eyes hold back every bit of bemoan spilling out of me.
Nobody sees me.
Nobody feels me.

Nobody shows up for me.
It's only up to me to provide what I need, which should be easy until…
I can't hold myself unless it's up.
I can't explain to myself why my life is so rough
around the edges.
I can't smooth this anger over.
I can't cover the emotions on my shoulders.
All this pain as I'm getting older, and it
just sits.

He used to look at me inappropriately, and some of the things he would say,.....
I knew he was invading a certain space where those boundary lines usually stay,
to keep him away
but I never said nothing
until one day he got to touching and his fingers
rubbing but he never got too close because of the things I know.
His true colors started to show, so I chose to tell about the last time.
Still, I should have spoken about every line fed
cause now I will never be heard.
Every word he said
was believable
looking in your eyes, claiming he's apologetic of getting too comfortable,
but I knew he watched my thighs, studied all my curves, and conversed with me about my pearl in between.
He said he had seen it before, and if I needed assistance, he wouldn't mind
behind closed doors.
We even talked about how I was made out to be a whore.
The things that came to mind when asked if I was sure that he touched me

I can still feel his hands reaching down my pants coming in contact with my pubic hairs.
He asked me if I shaved sometimes
keeping up with the time I spent in the bathroom.
Anyway,
since that day, I remain in shock of the decision to keep these secrets hidden in my brain
locked up like the way I kept myself at night.
Right is right and wrong is just put away so you don't see.
Since he didn't go inside of me
I'm curious, should his actions not be taken that seriously?
This time love was blinded by the desire of possessing a man.
The neglect
ignited this need to vent, because you didn't see that your husband touched me without my consent.
I knew the situation would be swept away like it never happened.
And what was covered up didn't get healed, and the comforting motherly love that was for me you allowed him to steal.
The trust I had for him or any other man can't even begin to feel real.
Sometimes throughout my day, I get this disturbing chill about what I went through with you two
after revealing his feelings.
HE ATTEMPTED TO CREEP THROUGH MY PANTS

AND GAVE ME HIS TEARS ASKING FOR FORGIVENESS AND ANOTHER CHANCE!
Years later I still wonder,
What about me?
Was I not of importance?

A mother's love is beautiful.
It is deep, it's real, and unconditional.
It cannot be duplicated, replaced, or unwanted, but it can be hidden.
A mother's love can appear nonexistent
or maybe it's just distant.
Now I'm confused by this love she has bruised me with.
It wasn't just me who did this.
Mothers make logical decisions and advisory recognition to survive the mission of raising me.
Cuts so deep in my heart she wounded me.
From the dull look on her face every night and every day.
I will never know how happy she was to have me.
The lack of a mother's love stabs me when the thoughts of it sinks in.
I could never choose her to depend on.
Instead, I was always in the presence of another heart that was hurting just as badly as mine.
So we coped together,
and created a love that was designed to be disgraceful, and it left the impression that I was ungrateful and that my choices were distasteful.
Especially my failure to appreciate your efforts to do a motherly job.
You see essentially mothers did what they were supposed to do.
Provided shelter, clothes, and food.
She made sure we got to school and made us abide by the rules,

kept us in church, and presented that God is more important than anything on this earth.
Round of applause to all of you
just for doing the things you were supposed to do.
Now your kids can be placed on this pedestal to do the right things, because you have bestowed all the right tools.
Accept you didn't.
Above and beyond for me was not beneficial, so to be smitten by you is justified.
No tears in your eyes from my pain.
No joy in your heart for any success I worked to gain.
No time at all for me to be trained
to stand on my own.
To not be afraid to be alone.
No affectionate emotions were ever shown.
Now
I am grown,
and the error of your parenting you can't seem to trace.
I'm easily influenced, attention seeking, just looking for someone to accept my ways
and sometimes I give off this cold shoulder probably because of the things I lack
and if we backtrack

it was your faulty love that you bruised me with,
so don't you think for a second!
That it was just me
who did this.

I don't have any strength to cry tears from my eyes
too battered and scorned.
Heart shattered and torn from life's circumstances.
Chances and opportunities wasted.
My mind races faster than my speech these days, but my actions stutter so my character is impaired.
My potential stays hidden and my talents are questioned.
The dream and priorities are off balance.
There's no living without having a way to live, so I'm stuck incorrectly giving
because I don't know what to give.
Taking is all I see happening to me.

It's too much to not want to cry.
Pain too big to not want to die,
but I'm alive and not dead and that should be enough.
To wake up and blindly
chase this bread is what the white man wants anyway.
The obligations are just waiting on my next payday to get their share.
Don't worry about me in my time of despair.
A new day draws breath .
Get up and just breathe.
Act like I don't hear, see, or feel them ganging up on me.
Look!
They are coming for me, but just breathe because no one else sees me.
I'm just stuck to breathe
and then I'm struck by the weight and all I can remember is to
breathe.

My wrist tingles.
Something is moving on the inside of me
in my veins
as if I needed to let it out.
Open and release.
Cut and expose.
Attempt to cease the pain that never goes away.

Between trying and not wanting to try.
Crying but I don't want to cry.
I don't know why these emotions are taking control of me.
I want you, but I don't want you to hold me.
Incompetent is what I feel but capable is all I have shown.
Strength is all I have grown, but the pain is still there.
You can't see it and you can't tell from the outside,
but the insides feel like hell.
All I want is to brawl,
in a ball
and just exist.

Words trampling through my head as I lay in this bed full of pain
It's only shared in this place
without a trace of evidence dropped in any other location.
I travel through the dirt and the gravel.
I glide and I hide my lows and my highs
a network on the inside of me streaming my emotions.
In both areas I'm going through the motions.
Suicidal thoughts get controlling.
Depression gets controlling, but my life I'm still holding on, praying long and strong that the rest of me believes I still belong.
Even though I feel alone even though my joy is gone
I still belong.
Every day is a little darker and my urges get a little harder, to let the blood drip from my veins with a note of people to blame,
but my spirit makes a claim to go another day.
I fight my body to go another way regardless of all things my mind would say.
These feelings go on a relentless spiral in my brain
unexposed and unexplained.
I seem misunderstood only because I don't understand.
Whose hand took aid in my mental state?
Who is responsible for taking my life away?
I can't possibly be the master of this catastrophe .
This is blasphemy to my identity
I cannot accept this to be me.

I already feel so guilty.
I live with so much pain and so much rage so many tears and endless fears of coming home to write that note with
"Dear so and so."
Breaking down my fears to live,and appear just to drown in these clustered thoughts.
being whipped by life itself with the conflicting confusion it has brought.
All of my health systems incapable of catching a grip contemplating to let this blood drip, and ending my life and this letter with;
It's your fault
and I am so sorry……..

This is to you
If you have thought about committing suicide
I know those feelings
and they are never hidden from the frontal lobe of your brain, but I want you to listen to what I'm saying.
Try to hear me.
That once was me, and I am here with you.
I know what it feels like too,
and you are not alone.
I promise that if you stay here with me, you will come out on the other side strong
and you will find the tribe in which you belong.
Please
hold on with me.
Wrap your arms around your body
left over right.
Squeeze yourself tightly,
keep holding, and breathe
Read these words and repeat;
"I am hurting and it is not okay,
but I will be intentional every day
to comfort me and improve my mental and emotional health
I love me; I will love me
because I am all that I need."

Chapter 4:
The Motions of the Condemned, and Convicted

Idk if it's my spirit or my anxiety or, something else somewhere,
where I can't reach
from the outside of me.
I'm fine.
I'm close to happy, but these tears I'm feeling is holding on
to something inside of me.
I don't know what's happening, but it's pulling on me.
I think it's on to me
and I just can't let go.
It's haunting me,
which is exactly what I asked for.
It's on to me in my sleep that I don't get, because it's there talking to me past dawn.
In my day it's on to me whispering Christian songs coming from my lips.
I didn't know it would happen like this.
It's on me.
It's on to me, then it's in me during the most inconvenient ambiance,
like when someone is jumping my bones
and it's on me.
The pressure gets on me to do everything right even though sometimes
I feel I'm doing nothing wrong
then it's on me.

It's catching up on me.
All these big and little feelings.
All these dealings.
I'm trying to light up to drown them out of me so they can be gone to me.
Solange said the cranes were in the sky,
but them shits are coming down on me.
I'm trying to stay distracted, but it's consuming me.
I'm trying to unpack it, but it's overloading.
I'm trying to tear it down,
but it has power over me.
I'm trying to kick it out, but it is crowding me.
The doctors say to medicate, but it's suffocating.
My mom is trying to erase it cause it's replacing me.
The therapist is trying to destroy what's taking over me.
I'm running, trying not to face it cause it's scaring me. I'm losing my breath.
I can't keep up.
It's on to me.
It got me.

You created me. You made me.
I am forever in debt to you.
All credit God, goes to you for everything you brought me through.
You favored me.
You savored me even when you didn't have to.
I am not worthy.
I fall short of doing your will, and in the midst of my guilt I still…..
I'm sorry.
If I could reach for this sin and take it out of my body
I would
rip it from my sinful flesh if I could.
I want to.
It would be better.
I would be great if I could look my sin in the face and walk away.
Walk on,
walk straight like your soldier and never looking over my shoulders with doubt
experiencing everything the saints say you're about.
They say it's not over until you say so, but God does that apply to all things that go.
You know me and every move I make.
My life to you is like your own video tape, so tell me.
Are you putting me through this sin to teach me a lesson?

I'm stressing because blessings still reach me even through my depression.
Excuse my expression if I come off defiant.
I'm just trying to understand my own self the way you do.
I feel my love for you shows despite my sins, but I am told otherwise by the Christian girls and guys.
It's all so confusing but amusing the way they judge.
I try to take hold of you when I'm tempted to hold a grudge.
God I'm misunderstood by this universe, but you get me.
You said it.
I'm sure it's some verse of the bible that I rarely read, but the goodness of your works I swear I speak.
Just please know even in my nature it's your face I always try to seek.

I pray sometimes at night
while I convince the world that I'm this good girl, but inside
I travel the path of darkness.
Gay love is the reason I will burn in hell?
This beautiful sin.
I wonder if I will ever gain the strength to fight the feeling within.
Gay love is a daily routine,
while profane language is only used to make a scene or put emphasis on words and things.
You will never understand it the way I do.
You will never have this fear in your heart from all the things that could be true.
I WILL NEVER NOT LOVE YOU.
YOU?
Gay love
is my shortcomings.
Gay love is my relief from stress.
My gasp of fresh air.
It's my paranoia when I light it up.
My pick me up when I'm down.
My everything
and all around.
It's my danger zone, and for that reason the devil can't leave me alone.

Home is exactly where this sin isn't, and for this sometimes my love gets distant.
For I know that the Lord has risen.
Baby we can't have forever.
I'm no actress, and we can't practice playing house
I can't have a woman as my spouse, because she is something that I must live without.
It makes me sick, you know.
This damn thing can feel just like a heartbreak sometimes.
The things that disturb my mind.
I'm cautious mentally, but physically I put gay love first.
I can't continue to put myself in this curse,
because that is the sin.
God is above all and ignoring him is like saying I want to fall,
or I want to fail.
This love was real, but it was wrong.
So, I leave you the memories to reminisce while I'm gone; because this love was real, but this love is wrong.
I'm sorry for dragging you this long.
You always had my heart.
When we depart I must take it back, so I can feel
When the Lord accepts my soul.

Wash me.
Wash me.
This debris,
wash me.
This thing is hurting.
Wash me.
This thing is burning,
just
wash me.
Wash
me.
It's no secret that the Lord has kept me
He swept me from the razor blade, alcohol, sex, and the girls that played
a role in my crazy.
The daisies are still so far away.
I pray everyday
it's a shame I still lack a little faith.
The pain is long-lasting.
It's dragging me into scary areas,
like the burial sight of my grave I created for myself.
I've lost my dignity that I'm not sure I ever had and it feels so bad
hiding how sad I am through my days of perkiness, in everyone's face
because I am more than a conqueror; in God's name.

So let the weak see that I am strong, just make sure they don't follow me home.
There's no guarantee that I can hold this facade for very long.
Mommy,
come hear me crying.
I feel like dying.
I know I have to keep trying.
The fear of failure is so accessible.
It sits at my pity table and tells me how I'm allowed to quit.
That there's another place where I can exist and not be SHIT.
I just have to do it.
Lay down my life, surrender to the strife and everything will burn like it's intended to.
I took an interest in all women that wanted to indulge in my sinning.
I imposed on their seasons just for my self-fulfilling reasons
as long as they were decent.
It was,
it is a real disease,
and internally I was displeased with being so easy
the lifestyle doesn't fit me.
My persona was a fabrication of me being happily
wrong.
In a room full of people I still felt alone
with family, my friends, my lovers and even songs.

I've tried everything I've known and remained solely on my own.
Desolating inside.
So, Lord I ask you
to guide me
and stay by my side please.
Stop my backsliding
so I can stop this lying,
and my flesh will no longer define me.
Then my walk will be amplified.
My words will be edifying.
My works will be gratifying,
and my praises will be more glorifying
God, my steps will be complying with your speech.
My love will be undying if you teach.
Father with you,
my bad habits will be rectified.
This time my salvation can be signifying
I insist that you persist in purifying
ME.
In Jesus name
Wash me.
Wash me.
I wanna be clean.
Wash me.

I said I wanna be free
God PLEASE WASH ME!
Amen

I feel weak in the knees.
Seeking God is not always easy;
between the he's and she's that come across me
touching my vulnerabilities.
Please make it stop, because my mouth can't even drop to say any words of dismissal or rejection,
or fight my wandering mind from affection that's not even guaranteed.
I can't plead with perfection,
nor can I fail this inspection of the things my heart is supposed to desire.
All this fire and passion
all this fire I'm attracting to my soul, lacking focus on the heavenly goals.
Who in the hell told my flesh to awake and refresh my obsession to be touched,
memorizing the rush of vibrations from skin to skin
rejuvenation reaching into my bones.
I've got the jones for that intoxicating,
can't catch my breath grazing
brush that makes me blush in the middle of the day kind of play,
but this can't stay.
I'm feeling some type of way about my types and about my ways and it ruins my day, but I still can't make myself say "it needs to go away".
This uninvited interruption

beginning an introduction to a chapter that I can't go after.
I fear the level of unknown disaster from this capture of a mere temptation to feel something sensationally temporary.
The scary results of a risk with previously experienced outcomes.
Yet and still my mouth, mind, and body
is still letting disruptions
walk all over me.

Lord forgive me for the thoughts of this sin.
It's dancing with the hair follicles on my skin
making them stand up, arousing my hormones from the thoughts to the messages that used to get sent to my phone.
Lord forgive me.
My mind is in a zone.
The moments just keep piling and piling, and I'm just-a smiling and-
Jesus!
SLAP ME IN MY RIGHT MIND!
These are not the kind of things I need to think about.
What is happening to me?
I know I'm still a sexual being, but Lord I need you to control some things.
You know what I'm talking about.
I guess I'm supposed to shout your name out loud
for you to remove these fowl escapades
from me when I once was a sinner and strayed from your love.
LORD!!
Destroy the wrong things my mind is thinking of.

Chapter 5:
When you fall for love

I don't want to tell you "love", and fail you
Love.
Even though your love is the very drug that arrested my heart, flesh, and wounds.
It caused me to resume this conscious unrevealed experience.
The clearance of my mind is honestly disturbed
by the curve ball you have thrown me for a comforter.
life circumstantial evidence advertised you as my protector.
I can't claim incompetence of retreating
from the way you are treating me.
The possibility of you keeping me has my anxiety going crazy.
I like how you crave me.
The attention you pay me with your creative intellect has phased me.
You draw me in closer on a daily.
MY GOD PLEASE SAVE ME!
I thought you were supposed to change me, but when I look at the face of Lady.
Her eyes chasing mines,
and thoughts of her tracing my mind.
I am glad to be tortured with this kind
of love.

You have rare love.
You care about love, so I ask you to share love with me.
Is this our destiny?
Are you soon going to be forever next to me?
It's scary
and I might add a little difficulty; but you pull out the best of me.
In my eyes when you look at me, I don't know what you see.
Flaws and all you remain to love me.
Through every season after three heart breaks you still have my love for keepsake.
I'm madly in love with you and you are with me too; and the things you do is everything to me.
It sends me a bliss inside and out.
I could never cease to know everything you're about.
And when my love seems to be of a drought,
You still extend forgiveness and replenish me for my shortcomings.
The forever's with you are frightening that's why I keep running.
There's no confusion about this feeling.
Your intimacy gives me some kind of healing.
Our chemistry adds up equally.
We got our history and I can comprehend it literally through your eyes, deeply bringing out heavy sighs from this exhaustion and second wind all in one breath.

You make me inhale love.
You let me come out of my shell, Love.
Your kisses put me on this drug affiliated inebriation.
With you I swear I can touch the sky.
With you your conversations are never dry,
 because you understand my intellect.
No one has topped you yet.
You been loving me from age 15
to 21 and I feel like our journey has just begun.
In the presence of you I have already won.
With you every moment is magical,
unfathomable is what this love is to me.
Not practiced or performed.
Far from fraudulent or concocted.
Never artificial.
Not just physical.
You have rare love.
You care love, so share Love.
Forever.
Even if we don't stay together.
It will always have been my pleasure.
To have you, so
Thank you.

It's like an all expense paid vacation when you make your way in
for the weekend.
It's no worries.
There are no hard decisions or reason to hurry.
I just get to laugh and let loose a little just for the weekend.
We could go anywhere or nowhere at all.
As long as we can look at each other, fall, and still catch one another.
Well until I get others involved.
We used to make extended stays, but there are stipulations to loving the impossible.
I know we like to think anything is possible, but this still remains unsolvable to me.
I can't see pass the things that control me
my mother, religion, and what other people think.
All equal control and not one having a stronger hold
on me.
Baby when I'm with you I'm just with you.
My own real fantasy,
so after the weekend my fantasy stops and I run away to reality.
I go home and I face the things that make me unhappy because I'm too afraid of the eternity that comes with loving
the impossible.

You are my high, and the downside of my goodbyes,
but with every hello there is a new beginning.
Your love is a trending topic all over my body and your kisses are a resilience to my emotions.
You soothe me.
With your eyes you move me to a place that is unknown to be retracted.
The pace of this reconnection is at an instant rate.
The traits you have to catch my attention could never be denied.
For as long as you desire, I'm always by your side.
Disconnecting this love, we have tried.
Missing you everyday I attempt to hide,
but now I choose to reveal the secret.
I know that you will forever keep it.
You are my weakness which I despise, but I need this.
I'm proud of my addiction.
I've overdosed on this prescription
and now I'm empty.
Will you refill me?

I have this thing about wanting to know you,
to see where your mind goes and watch the things you do.
Is it random, or does it all flow and make sense?
What makes you crack a smile?
What is your imagination like?
What would the experience feel like to see your inner world?
Can I come in?
Will you accept my request?
I mean I'm kind of nervous
about introducing you to my vibes, but there is this urgency of mine to let you accompany me.
Will you share your time with me and converse with me?
I want to see where your subconscious thoughts will take me.
Get me entangled in your brain.
I'm confident I can relate and find my way
I know I'm being silent. I just want to hear all your words that you don't say.

Chapter 6:
….And When it Crashes into you

The User and the Used
I caught you today
creeping up my skin
attempting to steal away my thoughts within
to take a shot at the spotlight in my mind.
What do you want?
Whatever it is I don't have it
and you already know this, it's not like we haven't
had this conversation before.
Are you bored?
Did you need some entertainment for today so you come by to laugh at
me run away
from you.
The thoughts of you.
The dumb ass desire to be with you.
Are you watching me stew over how I screwed you over?
I see you.
Did you want me to come over so I can screw you some more?
You want permission to use me as a distraction.
Take a crack at being me since I appear to be absent in your life.
Why are you bothering me?
Hasn't your heart reached its capacity of scratches and bruises left with
my initials

that I left initially to remind you of what I do so turn me loose; and dare not to play this game with me cause I promise you'll lose.

I hate waiting on you.
I like you a lot but not enough to fight for.
The emotions I go through wondering how much you will like me for today.
It's embarrassing for me to sit on the edge of my seat
and wait for you to greet me with some form of communication.
I should have never gotten into this situation.
I don't even want to feel like this!
Being your lesbian mistress.
Don't get it twisted, "I still love your kisses", and the mystery of being blessed with
the chemistry of your company,
It's amazing,
but my feelings get confusing when I'm waiting.
anticipating our meetings.
I swear.
I know you have a relationship, so this affair requires space that is why when I think about contacting you I hesitate.
Then I voluntarily choose
to wait……..

I psyched myself out thinking this would be a forever, or at least a little while thing..
I guess we were on different pages cause I assumed a little while would be longer.
I try to forget about your kiss, but one reminisce is all it takes to be pushed four steps back from the healing.
No! You're not the one to blame. How dare I fault you, or lie to say you lead me on.
You were pretty clear and headstrong about being in love with a man that can give you things I can't.
There's a fog about your feelings for me.
I guess that was kept a secret purposely to prevent this situation.
The complications of not knowing is stunting my growth away from you, because you refuse to tell me the truth.
At least the truth I believe.
You won't provide me with closure so my love for you grows closer and my actions get a little bolder either way.

When I see an Impala I think about ya,
but I'll learn to digress from the stress of not knowing how to get you off my mind.
Thoughts of you are overrated.
I'm not saying I hate it,
but if we both threw out an estimated number of times we were infatuated with each other
I already know whose would be greater. My obsession is tailored to every session with you.
I can countdown our heated moments.
In 3. When you rushed me with an unexpected side of you that we only talk about.
I felt your desired inquiries touch mines and set off my sacred outburst.
I tried to maintain playing this game with you.
Round 2. Showed up quickly you came in contact with pricklies in my panties and showed me you weren't ready.
Still you laid my back against your steering wheel facing the character from my dreams I used to have.
Grabbing for my addiction I catch you and the afflictions I knew this would bring me.
We both ignored it reaching under my clothes and another outburst of moans flowed into the air.

1. More time without crossing too many lines we admitted a wanting for each other's attention
face to face.
When there has been too much space I often get this way
like a junkie with a feen to be in between your seats experiencing the fire we make with our body heat.
Tending to your obligations of daily business, you stopped by for a "have a good day" kiss.
There was a want for more of me you expressed by using reverse psychology,
but off you had to go.
I left with fear of knowing that my countdown of moments with you has reached
0.
Now I stand here twiddling my thumbs
thinking about our last encounter and how it's all gone.
I didn't get that far with you, but the established distance was still unexpected.
It hurts to end this, but I'll accept it.
I would rather you be happy with your already established lifestyle than to destroy what you have with "lover boy"
just to walk this journey with me only to fulfill curiosities.
If you continued to be in this position with me

it could leave you in tears from reminiscing about what could be.
In addition,
I'm acknowledging that my feelings were getting too deep, and to think that you would take this long shot would be silly.
I once was a true believer that anything I wanted I could get, but despite the failure of not having you, there are still no regrets.
I enjoyed this short trip we engaged and to be able to talk about your lips on this page.
I will continue to dream about the many dips I could take between your hips with attempts to make you shake.
Like all great tales the time has come to an end
and as much as I would like to pretend, I prefer to be a better friend opposed to thinking this would never end.

For you, I do the most, and it's something I do like to boast about,
because I got a thing for you that runs through my veins.
Although I feel ashamed about it;
it's not a game when I say I love you.
From the moments we share and the gasps of air I try to retrieve in our space,
you can't tell me there's not a trace of love that you detect.
Even without the sex and you grabbing and kissing me, you still have me.
It's the intimacy I'll miss
, and I know there are numerous ways that I dissed you, but I'm not perfect.
I know you deserve the best of me, so you can't blame me for the hope that I have to no longer make you sad.
Deep inside of me resides some bad things, and you said you accept it.
I know I give your heart a little trouble and if you want me to remove myself from your bubble, I understand
but I'm doing the best I can.
I apologize for wanting to make future plans for me and you but I love you;
and that's why I do the things that I do.
I'm not good enough for you but it's hard to let go of the greatness that we have been through.

I Lied.
I cried numerous times
and I'm fond of repetition so
yes, I lied and so did you and somehow you think that shit is cool, but you're putting double standards on me.
Using your beauty to play with me, knowing damn well you never planned on staying with me.
Things have changed, so I can no longer play into your games you claim ignorance towards.
I try to be nice about it cause my love is still the same, but my mindset has been rearranged.
"Let's just be friends."
I can vent to you.
We can share laughs and giggles, but you can't give me mixed signals.
I'm not strong enough to diss you.
Yes, I still miss you, but I'm not dumb enough to address the issue.
As the wise man says "there's always a price to pay", and I can't afford another painful heartache that you won't care to fix so let's just start over.
Leave the past where it's at.
I can't go back to that.
I apologize if you don't understand.
You might not realize the things you be saying and sometimes I chime in and start playing

filling in the blanks to your flirtatious riddles,
entertaining you just a little, feeding into your subliminals about the visuals of us getting physical.
It seems fun and simple until I'm left pitiful,
and then things start to get difficult all from the reciprocals of yours,
mines,
our mixed signals.

I think I would be okay if I stop dreaming about you.
Maybe if I just scream it out of my system I would be through.
I just don't understand how you dismiss my feelings
you know
the ones I'm not supposed to have.
I just knew I should have never chased your ass.
This morning I woke up for the first time allowing the tears to flow from my eyes.
I became so dependent on even just receiving your communication.
I can only admit to myself that I gained an obsession over these relations.
You tasted and wasted everything
on my everything in this affair.
I can't even back track where all this came from.
I feel like I need a procedure done to get our relationship surgically removed from my body.
This mind of mine is stuck on you all the time
entirely too much, more than I can handle.
I feel abandoned by your lips.
Tell me.
How do I get out of this shit?
These are my thoughts that I would never come to you with; because like me they will just remain unattended too.

I couldn't have you.
You're not mines,
and the laughter sickens me
making fun of my feelings about this fairytale that doesn't end too well.
From beginning to end it's tragic, but my desires for you still remain.
Wasted time is the least of my concerns because my mind still yearns for you
After a long day,
To be in my bed with a million things you could say that I know would make me smile.
For a little while
I could cater to you.
I could learn about all the things you went through and work overtime to make up for pain.
Hunger of wanting you close to me is the most overwhelming.
Anger
curiosity,
but the hurt is death threatening and it's obvious you don't care to resuscitate me.
You don't want to look into this case.
You still can't tell me why this started in the first place.
You still can't tell me
Why me?

Is it because you knew I would get attached emotionally
and your every feeling could control me?
Is it because you knew I couldn't let go
and I would continue holding on?
When the night comes, I hold my pillow tight as if it was you to get through the night, but
in the morning my dreams hurt more than when it feels good cause in reality
you're not actually with me the way I think you should be
and it's not so real anymore.
Thinking about you gets redundant
cause all this love I send your way just gets handed back to me
politely.
I know you mean no harm by not being in my arms,
but I wish you did.
Maybe it would open my eyes and rid of all the things I love about you
your attitude, your smart mouth and beautiful skin, and a bunch of other things I miss.

I positioned myself 10,000 times
trying to hold me like you once did,
and slowly I learned that anything remotely close to you
never works out as planned.

Tell me what you know about me and I will tell you what I know about you;
and how I know that it's all true
so don't disregard or try to break my heart with your lies.
Everything has been revealed in your eyes since way back then.
Once upon a time when we had that good kind of tension
I didn't listen to what my mind told me.
Somethings I ignored because I was more interested in exploring your heart and the things you would never share.
Those feelings you would never spare
out of the sake of security for yourself.
Even if you wanted to,
certain things with me you just wouldn't do
which I respect and resent,
because of the countless times I spent on trying to break into your shell.
This love spell has scarred me and I know you can tell that I can't let go, you keep me on this flaccid rope to make me dance for you at your convenience.
I'm persistent, because I know I could do you some good.
The things that I would do to make you smile if you weren't in such a denial of our love.
Together we could grow
if you show me the things I already know,

or convince me I'm wrong and close these open wounds you gave me with my permission.
It was a reckless decision I will never forget.
A journey I will never regret.
There is this instinct set upon me that won't leave well enough alone.
Tell me a thousand times that I am wrong and I will still feel our secrets we never show.
So tell me what you know about me.
I will tell you what I know about you
with a desire for confirmation that what I know is true.
That you do love me, and I am what your heart needs, and it has chosen me and my capabilities of healing you.
Just say its real cause your eyes reveal it all, but if the love is gone and my intuition is all wrong
Then please refrain from stringing me along and let go of the power of holding me at your fingertips.

Let me know when you are finished with that knife
carving your name in my heart
so I can put it away,
and keep it safe,
and hidden
from anyone that ever tries to do that shit again.

Chapter 7:
Manipulated and Manipulator

I liked it but I didn't.
The pleasure was there but the unpleasantry was also
sitting.
It was in arms reached,
but you kept going
deeper.
It made me weaker.
I couldn't say no or stop for numerous reasons.
Heavy breathing, eye engagement, skin to skin contact
I couldn't keep my thoughts intact.
In fact, it caused me to react to what feels good
and I couldn't detach from the current ambiance.
This is where the addiction comes in.
The sex and the sin can cause me to let you in,
and expect it again and again.
Then after
I begin to self-destruct
and look for you to build me back up
piece by piece.
At Least until I disagree with the parts that you try to make apart of me,
then I disagree and tell you what I really think.
It will seem as if I wasn't genuine with my feelings
which isn't true.

I'm always genuine with my feelings when I'm inside of you.
I just get a little distracted too,
and so I don't really think
 I just do
and think later.
I have to come up with something safer,
because this is how I cause my heart to waiver
and possibly do
something major that causes damage
and in the end
 one of us
will feel like
one of us has been taking advantage.

It was warm the way pain feels,
and the love
was covered in
sacrificial red blood
as it should be.
The tender spots were more tender and the tough spots turn soft,
then my eyes rolled back to the satisfaction of the blade on your tongue
that hypnotizes me.
Blood, spit, sweat, water, cum, and rain.
They all roll down our bodies the same way,
but my love
will choose what it wants
and it doesn't have to look like yours.

I don't want to pretend anymore.
I want to be yours.
Are we even really friends' baby;
or am I just playing your whore?
If you say yes
I still won't walk away.
You caused me so much pain and all I want is more,
so come and give me my scars
and reopen my sores.
I'm addicted to your shit.
It was always supposed to be like this anyway.

The ugly truth.
Most people would refuse to acknowledge it.
Hell I'm even against it;
but my conscience
overrides my ego sometimes
intensely taking over my mind
to the point of insanity.
It's restraining me.
Revealing the ugly truth will make me lose everything.
Ugly truth?
The ugly truth is
you're so freaking ruthless
inconvenient, and useless.
Why are you doing this?
The ugly truth is,
I deserve EVERYTHING I want.
The ugly truth
for you
I'm just pretty to flaunt.
The ugly truth is
I'm willing to lay down and allow you to step on me
cause I know I will be the beneficiary.
You will be taking care of me simultaneously

while I care for you.
Ugly truth is
Why should we let this ugly truth
destroy what we both are willing to go through
to get through?

You got that big love
that "Where you going without me" love.
"Don't sit down across the room I want you around me" love.
That
"Come to me first to cradle your insecurities'' love.
Your expression is bigger than me, so you come off as
superior love.
Your heartaches are equal to an earthquake.
When you're upset, the whole room shakes from your pain being heard
love.
You like to control me,
but you put it
in code for me
like it's just a strong suggestion;
but that shit is just getting old to me.
I got that loud love.
That hot and cold love.
It's sometimes unrelatable
hit or miss.
You can't pick which way to go love.
Between feeling unwanted and not wanting it
I got that complex love.
That " I'm not gon let you play me, I'm too proud" love.

I'll give you anything you want to shut your mouth love.
Sometimes I need space to breathe, cause your kind of love gets heavy especially in my weak moments.
So when you're throwing a tantrum this " I don't give a fuck" attitude really means
I care it's just not showing the way you want it to,
and stroking your ego is not something I want to do.
We got that competitive love.
That whose circumstances are greater than love.
You like to scream and shout, and it silences me out so I cry and pout;
and baby soon we get too exhausted to fight so we fake forgive .
We kiss lips and hold each other tight; and pull strength to try another day.
Yeah.
We got that crazy love.
That "I don't wanna stay, but I don't wanna go" love.
That hazy, no that lazy, I mean that soiled love.
That
"You waited too long to jump in, and I waited too long to jump out."
Now it's spoiled love,
and then all that love just floats away.

You use to love me in many different ways
and our relationship was more than what I can say on these present days.
You've opened my eyes to numerous things.
You secretly killed some of my precious dreams.
You made me not trust again.
Your bullshit turns me against my future lovers and second guess every other person in my life,
because they often remind me of you
with some of the sorry things you used to do.

I hate you,
but I also replicate you.
It's crazy how you loved me and loathed me at the same time.
You loved me and you loathed me with the same lies.
You touched me and you showed me how to let my soul burn.
I heard your "I cut myself" stories a million times then eleven lines appeared on my skin.
You manipulated me and I manipulate everyone over and over again.
I'm drowning in the sin that you taught.
I got caught loving you and my mind told me to stop,
but the attention you gave me.
The affection I craved was deep in the burdens
you laid inside my heart.
Seeking for a fresh start is the only way I can get through and move passed,
my past.
I hope these tears won't last.
I hope this pain won't last.
I hope these cuts go away.
I pray that one day,
I'll stop being you.

Chapter 8:
The Spiritual Realm

He blesses me
but he cuts me the deepest.
His sheep is
always around
to defend his almighty power.
I am his daughter and he is my father; so I'm sure feelings are mutual.
I'm told that I'm created in his image,
but when I look at me there are a few blemishes.
All the while I look at him and see the same for this perfect God.
Like how I feel him most when I'm right and he seems to catch ghosts
when I'm a little wrong.
The times where I need him close and he's just gone or I'm just wrong.
Either way the pain is still as strong as the power.
Powerfully strong, wrong,
And gone.
My complaints may be long, but it doesn't mean I don't love him.
I still defend him first
instead of relating to my brother or sisters hurt
like most of us do.
I call his name!
If his love is better than mine why can't he do the same?
I was taught to speak when spoken to, but I learned that christians are
"the church" to release what you have been going through.

I sense a few contradictions.
I mean I don't fully think his word is fiction.
I'm just saying we are made in his image.
Is it possible God may have a blemish or 2?
I'm quite angry with my father and I'm sure he's disappointed in his daughter.
Our behavior sometimes seems to bother one another, but it's starting to really get under my skin.
When does this family feud end?
I'm just sick of being confused.
Where are you inside of me; and how do I reside in you?
Doubtfulness is not what I want to feel about your existence, but I feel like we should be coexisting with each other.
It is said that your love is greater than any other.
You all break my heart the same.
Forgive us this day.
Teach me to forgive you one day, and show me you in a different way because today all I can say is
My father
he blesses me
but he cuts me the deepest, and although I can be a disappointment as a daughter
REGARDLESS
He promised that he would pick up the pieces.

What is the right description of this God above?
Is it our interpretations, or is it just what other people speak of?
When seeking WISE counsel our words usually amount to
something that could never be equal
to what he really is.
I want to take a moment and review the message we give.
Love God.
Do right.
Go to heaven.
You can have confessions, but it can't be re-run sessions.
Oh and always die I mean strive for perfection.
It is when we do these things we will start to feel a connection with the messiah.
Is this the only thing he accepts?
Is this what he requires?

I am not always full of courage.
I don't always feel encouraged, but I wasn't taught to be comfortable enough to let you be invited;
so I hide it. I disguise what's on my insides even though you are inside.
I still hide, then I start to despise myself.
I try to die to self .
Thinking of suicide to crucify the lies when I say "I'm ok."
"I'm blessed and highly favored." "This is the day."
I'm taking these ques from your chosen people, but all I want to do is speak the truth.
Yes you are the Way, the Truth, and the Light, but God first I need to share my insight of life.
I need to be raw with you about the emotions I go through.
Tell me that this is allowed.

So I'm smoking on this black and mild because this world is bringing me down and I only wish to talk to you.
To speak what's inside my head, and share the thoughts that cuddle me in my bed.
I wish that you could be my best friend.
I'm convinced then that all this guilt and shame would end.
If I could open up to you, tell you the pain I go through.
I'm weak when I settle for whoever gets between these sheets.
It's taking a toll on me.
The secrets I keep
and the attention I seek from these girls.
I could parse in a million different ways.
My emotions are downhill.
The thrill that spills inside comes only for a second.
So can we talk?
Could you take this walk with me as I reveal myself?
If you say yes,
could you make it easy?
Would you hold back your righteousness and just see me?
Can I conquer fear and allow myself to speak?
Do you have any questions to ask
about my choices in the past?
Could you listen without judgement?

Will you understand and continue to hold my hand while I struggle and slip.
I'm trying to tighten my grip but I still slip
but I beg and plead.
I'll beg on my knees.
Don't
leave
me!
Please!
Listen when I speak
open minded with unlimited timing
because there's so much to say
and it won't happen all in one day.
It actually may be a life journey
and honestly
I'm not sure I can do this, but if I have you I can try to commit.
So could you be
my best friend and listen
and love me no matter what.
when I'm finished.

Drake once said he was in-between psychotic and iconic and I get it.
I'm between a sinner and a christian, but I have good intentions.
It could be said that I'm not meeting the standards required
I try my best
but I have messes that cause me to have to reset and try again.
Start from the beginning and sometimes there is still a little sinning.
The church say the first step is admitting
and then I fall on my knees for the repenting and get back up
only to have the same sinful mind.
I mean is there anyone that got it right on the second or seventeenth time.
Granted the crimes I make against you may look a little different from most religious people
So does that make me a disgrace? Does it disgust you to see my face?
When life has me desperate and low and I go to what I know to cope?
Am I excluded from your grace.
I don't condemn the way I am because that's not my place, but the religious world makes me feel misplaced.
Do I fit in as your child?
I mean I get wild. I get loud . I get crazy. I can be a little lazy and selfish and sometimes I fear to share the gifts I've been blessed with.
The love I give is a little twisted because sharing it with the misses is a little sweeter than with the opposite.
God, let me put it like this

I know I have better potential but sometimes I really seek you in the physical
I need my father.
In this world life only gets harder.
Parental absence is the hardest lesson to learn twice.
If I could just touch you and rest on your chest every so often
being in a coffin wouldn't scare me, not making it through your gates wouldn't despair me and I wouldn't be overwhelmed with the burdens I carry.
So yeah sometimes you watch me slacking but can you make your mercy everlasting.
I'm just trying to make it through without thinking of the things I'm lacking.

Lord,
I hold pillows in my bed with wishful thinking in my sleep
that you would just come lay next me.
I'm really not understanding how this goes.
Am I supposed to hide my hurt and pain?
Can you please explain who am I supposed to be vulnerable with?
Everyone has their own shit they want to unload and I have taken a boat load with all the listening I have been giving at the time
but it can never be returned when I have some things in mind
to release.
I'm asking you to extend me some peace.
I don't want to request anything that is not in your plans
but I do need to place my thoughts in your hands.
You are the only one that will remember and listen to everyone
You are where my Help comes from, but when is my help going to come?
Like Adam and Eve, when will I get to see the rib that I was made from?
My loneliness is getting deeper and
I'm desiring my leader to keep me in your light
I'm not ready to be a wife, but I want to get to know the lover of my life.

The Middle,
they say there is no such thing even though the word was created.
The Middle.
A lukewarm christian.
It sounds like noise with no official comprehension
and you can't tell where it's coming from,
because you don't know how you got in;
It feels lonely because someone has forgotten to tell you about it.
It's the gray area.
It's blurred and foggy like a hazy smoke session and it doesn't feel bad;
but it doesn't feel good either.
It's right before you get to the darkness and when you realize the darkness is different you get right back to
The Middle,
the gray area.
We should call it the stay area because that's exactly what it's designed to make you do.
Stay.
The people that got out don't want to come in, so you experience isolation right next to the others in solitude
and don't know how to help each other because
we didn't talk about the gray area.
Some of us were just born in it, and we adapted but nobody taught us how to leave.

I'm outraged in this cage.
Let me out!
I want to walk around.
I want my sounds to be heard. I want everyone to know I exist.
In the midst of your daily agenda
I'm hindered,
but I exist inside you screaming this beautiful tune.
I assume you are not intrigued by my presence.
That you encourage my absence and disregard my "nonsense", cause it's unrelatable to you.
I am spiritual, but your religious ritual keeps me in this box.
I'm restricted to live my intentions only throughout these four corners and the borders are the main reasons I cross the line.
It's so much exposure during this day and time and "the church" tells you not to engage
IF I can't explore then how will I know what I worship God for?
If he is all powerful, all, knowing, and all seeing then why am I constrained to a sheltered being?
Doesn't that make me an easy target regardless?
Isn't it our fathers wish for us to go out and influence others of his way, truth, and light
Your way might not be the right approach for me,
so take these shackles off my feet and release me from your religious strait jacket.
I WANT TO BE FREE!

And that also means free from your outdated beliefs that Jesus himself died to relieve us from.
This religious cage has done nothing but feel me with rage, doubt, and unshameful sin
because of the fear you had me sitting in I walked away from my God many times.
I let the church control my mind and don't get me wrong
somethings were good foundations to stand on,
but the rest I have to discover on my own.
The way is a path only completed through crazy faith.
Faith I'll have as I open the door to leave this box
and grab the key to
lock myself OUT.

I'm mad, sad, and confused with you, God
Yep
I said it and it can be explained
because I been through somethings I don't understand,
and the things I've done
I can explain.
I just didn't think I had to,
so God while you've been mad with me
I've been mad at you!
I mean the things you make me go through with no explanation
why is it when I give reciprocation
I'm rewarded with condemnation?
You understand what I do and what I go through
Well God I think I deserve some understanding too.
From manipulation and molestation to abandonment
and somehow I'm expected to live with good intent
and practice forgiveness towards the ones that betrayed me.
God I don't approve of this life that you gave me.
I can't give you one time I didn't feel alone.
Even when I did my wrongs
to fill the void, you left me with in the first place
I still look for ways to fill the space where you are supposed to be.
It's not easy and I know it wasn't meant to be

but when are we going to come to agree?
I've experienced death, depression and denial.
My actions were reactions of the men and women that defiled me
I was coping.
I've been moping and crying hoping that you would save me from dying in my attempts to kill myself.
Then you introduced me to mental health just to take me through darkness to "heal" it all.
I FEEL FUCKING LOST!
I'm out here in the wilderness using the stars and signs to direct me home
and you still have me all alone.
How much wrong have I done that led to this suffering?
You said when I repent all is forgiven,
so why do I have to face these punishments with endurance?
I know afterwards comes your blessing,
but do we ever get to discuss these lessons?
Will you answer any of my questions or do I just blindly follow your direction always?
And when will all this hurt go away?
I'm mad, and sad, and confused with God
but I don't wanna be
I just want to really start to feel him walking with me.

I started talking to God when I learned no one else is listening.
It might feel like silence,
but his response is through intuition.
When I stand firm against flesh confliction
I start to see my harvest come to fruition.
In my prayers and meditation I can align my manifestations with his plans
and sometimes I do feel him holding my hand
as long as I don't let go.

I just want to succeed.
I just want to succeed.
I just want to succeed.
I just want to succeed.
To succeed
is where all my energy goes toward.
Manifesting to move upward and forward.
I just want to succeed.
I'm on my knees
praying "Lord please."
The confidence I need only comes from his glory, and if I succeed people will see the God in me.
That works for me,
through me,
with me.
Then who can be against me when I succeed.
When I succeed I promise not to be tainted by money and greed.
When I succeed I will use my influence to get people to believe
that in order to succeed you have to be one with the king.
You have to come to agree with the almighty in order to have the life of eternity.
The focus is not the things that are temporary.
The material.
The monetary.

That's all great, but the kingdom living through his gates
That's what I mean when I say
I just want to succeed.

Oh oh the places you'll go.
The things you see, and the things they'll show.
Some of it is color.
Some of it is plain.
It will make you think.
It will make you change.
Oh oh the people you meet.
Some of them lie.
Some of them cheat.
Some people are good.
Some people are bad.
They will make you happy, and they will make you sad.
Oh oh the person you are.
You've been through dark times
that made you a star.
You've shed some tears.
You've had some smiles.
Everything that has been
 was only for a while.

Thank you to all.
Love,peace, and light to you

www.ingramcontent.com/pod-product-compliance
Lightning Source LLC
Chambersburg PA
CBHW022115090426
42743CB00008B/858